The Career Vectors System
Basic Version

CVS Self-Assessment Process | CVS Summary Profiles

CareerVectors

Barry Lustig, M.A., Prof. Dipl.
Developer of the Career Vectors System

Hope Lovell Newman, L.M.S.W.
President, Career Vectors, L.L.C.

Table of Contents

General Introduction

The 21st century economy and labor market is fast-changing, increasingly global, and technologically driven. To navigate the 21st century means being able to keep up in a world of constant change.

In this turbulent and changing world of work we know today, the process of career decision-making has become, for many, more complex and confusing. Career planning and decision-making in these increasingly competitive, rapidly changing and uncertain times can present many challenges. Predicted trends for the future indicate that Americans will change jobs, even careers, several times over the course of their working lives. Because of this, periodic self/career exploration and assessment and ongoing career management have become essential to career survival, success and satisfaction.

The need for flexibility, perseverance, resilience, and adaptability along with planning, lifelong learning, and continual self-development is greater today than ever before.

Many people enter careers by accident, or take the path of least resistance, then later find themselves growing increasingly dissatisfied for a whole host of reasons. But, they are often confused about what to do next.

People today are also frequently faced with the need to find a new career direction because of layoffs, mergers, globalization, the speed of technology, and other factors beyond their individual control.

College students and working adults in transition, in order to further their career development, need to understand their work-related strengths and development needs, personality characteristics, and motivational factors (interests, values, and needs) as well as their career options.

All of these people would benefit from increased understanding of themselves, self-development, and greater occupational knowledge as a foundation to facilitate their search for a meaningful career direction, to make more informed career decisions, and to manage their careers more effectively.

This is the purpose of the Career Vectors System.

Introduction to the Career Vectors System
Basic Version

Welcome to the Career Vectors System (CVS) Basic Version — a career assessment instrument designed to provide you with information about your vocational interests, strengths and development needs, work-related personality characteristics, and occupational possibilities to explore.

This version of the CVS contains fifteen clusters in each scale of vocational interests, occupational preferences, skills, and personality traits.*

In the CVS, the term Career Vector refers to a broad career direction or orientation. In this system, the world of work is divided into six Career Vectors. The six Vectors may be thought of as global career themes that indicate specific career directions within the world of work.

Each Vector is characterized by certain personal characteristics and each person has varying degrees of Career Vector preferences.

Another version of the CVS, the Comprehensive Career Assessment Version is also available which is a more lengthy, detailed version that is made up of twenty clusters of vocational interests, occupational preferences, skills, and personality characteristics. It also contains more in-depth information in each section and will be available online. For more information, please see our website at www.careervectors.net.

The terms CVS and CVS Basic Version will be used interchangeably.

Goals of the CVS Basic Version

Upon completing the CVS, you will have undertaken a review of major factors that contribute to your career success and satisfaction including your interests, skills, personality characteristics, and strengths and development needs, as well as possible career options to explore.

Hopefully this information will help you further your career development and help you achieve the following goals:

1) A clearer sense of who you are in work/career related terms and a better understanding of your career potential by knowing who you are and what you have to offer.

2) The CVS can help facilitate self-exploration and career exploration. It can provide a process to facilitate more informed career decision-making/career choice and a possible reduction in career confusion. This can be achieved through greater self-understanding and knowledge of yourself, and an expanded awareness of suitable career options and possibilities to explore.

3) To enhance your personal and professional effectiveness by fostering an understanding of your strengths and development needs.

4) Enhancement of your marketability and job search effectiveness through understanding and being able to articulate what you have to offer prospective employers in terms of the kind of person you are and your strengths, skills and abilities, and work-related personality characteristics.

5) Career management is critical to success in today's economy and workplace. The CVS can provide a foundation of meaningful self-knowledge and career awareness to enable you to be more effective in the ongoing planning and management of your career.

Directions

Based on your reading of the characteristics of each Career Vector described in the next section, choose the three Career Vectors that you believe you resemble the most and which hold the greatest degree of appeal for you. Starting with these three, go through each scale following the directions indicated. Next, if time permits, complete the remaining Career Vectors, especially the personality sections which have the most general application.

At the end of each Career Vector scale, you will have an opportunity to record your results in the summary table provided. There, you can list your results on each of the four sections that make up each Career Vector; namely your career-related interests, preferred occupations, current motivated skills and potential skills, and work-related personality characteristics.

After you have completed three or more scales, please transfer all of your Summary Table results onto the Overall Summary of Career Vector Results on page 58.

Following the Overall Summary of Results, there will be a group of Summary Profiles for you to record and prioritize your most significant Career Vector data.

These Summary Profiles are designed to highlight some key aspects of your career-related characteristics and strengths and weaknesses. They will provide you with a record of your CVS results that you can use as a future reference as you plan and manage your career.

Please bear in mind, however, that you do not have to complete all the Career Vector scales and do the summary profiles at one time. You can do one Vector scale at a time, if you wish, and then return at a later time to complete the others.

The Six Career Vectors

In the CVS, people's career orientation and the world of work are divided into the following six Career Vectors (broad career orientations and themes) as originally developed and named by Dr. John Holland (Making Vocational Choices, 1997), whose work provided the foundation for the Career Vectors System.

Holland believed that individuals and work environments could be characterized by six vocational personality types which we call Career Vectors. Each Career Vector can be thought of as a cluster of personal characteristics that form a broad orientation to the world of work.

Each of the six Career Vectors has a characteristic pattern of vocational interests, preferred activities and occupations, skills and abilities, and personality characteristics. These characteristics are covered in some depth in the section on the Career Vectors scales on pages 14-57.

No person completely shares all of the characteristics of any one Career Vector. Most people resemble and share some of the characteristics of more than one Career Vector. However, usually one Vector is preferred, is most dominant and tends to determine the primary direction of career choice.

The CVS assessment is meant to help you determine which Career Vectors (career orientations) best describe you in order to help you better understand your own characteristics and strengths and weaknesses. It can also help you identify possible career directions you might wish to explore.

The following are the characteristics associated with each of the six Career Vectors:

#1: Realistic Career Vector

People in this Vector like to work with their hands, are often mechanically inclined, and like to build, construct, and make things. They frequently like to work with tools, machines, mechanical equipment and work that involves practical, hands-on problems and solutions.

They enjoy troubleshooting and solving mechanical and technical problems, and often like to fix and repair things such as cars, home appliances, aircraft, and biomedical equipment. They may also get satisfaction from repairing malfunctioning computers and providing technical support and assistance to computer users.

They tend to like to work outdoors and be physically active and often enjoy athletic and/or horticultural/agricultural activities such as growing plants and flowers and ranching/farming.

Occupations of interest include: automotive engineer, horticulture, solar energy systems designer, wildlife control agent, industrial arts teacher, building facilities manager, computer user support specialist, engineering technology specialist, computer systems hardware engineer, radiologic (x-ray) technologist, general building/home construction/home remodeling contractor, forest and conservation technician, airline and commercial pilot, and police/military officer.

#2: Investigative Career Vector

People in this Vector are interested in the life sciences (e.g. biology and genetics), the physical sciences (e.g. chemistry and physics), the medical/health sciences and the behavioral/social sciences (psychology, anthropology, sociology, economics, and political science).

They like work activities that involve investigating/researching, observing, analyzing, understanding and solving problems of a scientific, medical/health, mathematical/computer science, environmental, economic and/or of a psychological/behavioral/social science nature.

They have analytical abilities and often possess technical, scientific and/or mathematical skills and competencies. They also like working with ideas, concepts, and theories, enjoy work requiring abstract, and conceptual thinking, and like to explore and try to understand things.

They like reading about how the body works, medicine, health, nutrition, and new developments in the treatment of disease.

They tend to be interested in technology and systems-related work such as information technology and information systems and enjoy applying their knowledge to solve business and professional problems.

They also often like using computer science skills and/or quantitative analysis, mathematical and statistical techniques to analyze and solve problems and may enjoy teaching math and science at a high school or college level.

Occupations of interest include: STEM-related careers (science, technology, engineering, and mathematics/computer science), biologist, pharmacist, science teacher, computer systems analyst, chemical engineer, physician, optometrist, network and computer systems administrator, nutritionist, IT consultant, research and experimental psychologist, neuroscientist, neuropsychologist, computer network engineer, biomedical researcher, economist, and market research analyst.

#3: Artistic Career Vector

People in this Vector have an interest in artistic activities and occupations that provide outlets for their creativity and opportunities for self-expression.

They enjoy expressing thoughts and feelings creatively through various artistic media such as art forms and design, the performing arts, (e.g. music, dance, film and drama), the applied arts, (e.g. photography, interior design, and multimedia design including game design and development) and writing.

They like using imagination, innovation, and intuitive abilities and enjoy creating, designing, and developing new products, systems, and programs and coming up with new ideas, methods, and strategies to do things.

They like to work in unstructured settings and often enjoy visiting art exhibits/galleries, antique shops, museums, and attending concerts, the theater, and foreign films.

Occupations of interest include: advertising, photography, English/art/language teacher, journalist, multimedia (e.g. radio and TV), filmmaking, corporate communications, public relations, creating computer games and music videos, web designer, arts administrator, online content writer, book/magazine editor, graphic designer, architect, musician, art director/dealer, creative arts therapist, fashion designer, and digital media specialist/social media producer.

#4: Social Career Vector

People in this Vector like to help others, and gain satisfaction from activities such as advising, counseling, mentoring, providing social work services, and guiding, supporting and developing others.

They tend to be empathic, sensitive, nurturing and responsive to the needs, feelings, and concerns of others, and have a strong interest in their own and others personal growth and development.

They get satisfaction from helping others learn, and enjoy teaching, tutoring, training, and educational activities.

They frequently are interested in helping people deal with mental health issues and gain satisfaction from promoting individual and family mental health and well-being.

They also often get satisfaction from treating, healing, nursing, rehabilitating and improving the overall health and wellness of others.

They enjoy understanding, helping and counseling others and often have an interest in working with and helping children, the disabled, and/or the elderly.

Occupations of interest include: teacher, reading and learning disabilities specialist, occupational/physical therapist, college academic advisor/admissions counselor, minister/priest/rabbi, career counselor, social worker, applied psychologist, psychotherapist, nurse, clinical dietician, speech therapist, life coach, clinical gerontologist, vocational rehabilitation counselor, hearing loss specialist, certified diabetes educator, college student development specialist, special education teacher and child/senior center director.

#5: Enterprising Career Vector

People in this Vector often have business-oriented interests and enjoy solving business problems and negotiating business transactions. They like to manage people, programs, and projects, and like being in charge and leading, directing, and managing others.

They also like influencing and persuading others and selling and promoting products, ideas, and/or services.

They frequently have entrepreneurial interests and enjoy starting, operating and managing their own business or buying a franchise.

They tend to like activities such as helping organizations manage their computer and IT systems and resources, strategic business planning, management consulting, marketing (including e-commerce, internet, and social media marketing,) business development activities, and helping people and organizations with legal problems.

They also often have an interest in finance, investments, real estate, venture capital, and the management of money, financial assets, and financial resources for individuals and organizations.

Occupations of interest include: human resources manager, lawyer, real estate broker, business executive, investment fund manager, business school professor, entrepreneur, public administrator, management consultant, medical and health services manager, financial manager, purchasing manager, investment advisor/financial planner, environmental sustainability manager, real estate developer, computer and information systems manager, hotel manager, college and university administrator, non-profit agency manager, foreign service officer, sales manager, industrial/organizational psychologist, and executive coach.

#6: Conventional Career Vector

People in this Vector are often interested in practical business functions such as accounting, auditing, budget management, financial analysis, banking, quality control, business operations, and general administrative functions.

They like to work with data, specific information and detail as opposed to abstract ideas and general concepts.

They enjoy structured, detail-oriented activities and like developing efficient procedures for getting things done. They also enjoy bringing systems, order, structure and organization to the workplace to enhance efficiency, productivity, and keep things running smoothly.

They tend to like keeping things organized, working with and managing data, records, and information, and working with numbers and business oriented computers.

They may also like to meet the accounting needs of individuals and organizations, plan and manage budgets, and like analyzing financial information and preparing financial statements and reports.

They enjoy activities and roles involving the collection, organization, and practical use and application of data, and factual information for business purposes and/or to help people.

Occupations of interest include: accountant, auditor, database administrator, budget analyst, computer security coordinator, investment analyst, paralegal, librarian, insurance underwriter, web administrator, health information management specialist, real estate appraiser/title examiner, quality control specialist, credit analyst, legal research specialist, regulatory affairs specialist, professional organizer, quality control coordinator, business/ office manager/administrator, banking operations specialist, loan officer, special event, meeting and conference planner, social and human services assistant, and financial aid counselor.

#1: Realistic Career Vector

Section One: General Career-Related Interests and Preferences

Please review the clusters of career-related interests and preferences below. Check the box provided if any of the interest activity statements appeal to you.

• If some but not all of the activities mentioned within each box interest you, check the box and underline the particular activities that appeal.

• Don't hold back just because you don't believe you have the skills, education or training needed to perform the activity. If the appeal is there, check the box. Even if you have never performed the activity, if you think you would enjoy it, check the box.

1. I enjoy working with my hands and using mechanical and technical abilities to fix and repair things.	
2. I like to tinker with mechanical and electronic things. I enjoy taking them apart and putting them back together.	
3. I like to build, construct and make things and enjoy building and renovating houses and home improvement/remodeling activities.	
4. I like to be physically active and doing things.	
5. I would enjoy teaching courses in industrial arts, engineering technology, and/or computer repair.	
6. I like occupations providing security and protective services for people including law enforcement, police work, and military occupations.	
7. I would get satisfaction from providing technical support and assistance to computer system users.	
8. I like working with, training, and caring for animals.	
9. I like working with tools, machines, and mechanical equipment.	
10. I like seeing things grow and taking care of plants and flowers. I would enjoy working in a botanical garden.	
11. I have an interest in agricultural activities like farming and ranching and would enjoy owning and operating an organic farm.	
12. I like working outdoors and would enjoy careers such as the National Park Service, wildlife management, the environmental field, and outdoor recreation.	
13. I like working on and solving mechanical and technical problems and would enjoy trouble-shooting and repairing computer equipment and/or medical diagnostic equipment.	

(continued on next page)

(continued from previous page)

14. I would get satisfaction from being responsible for the facilities management and the overall maintenance, upkeep, and repair of buildings.	
15. I would enjoy owning and operating a state-of-the-art diagnostic automotive repair center and using the latest automotive technology.	

Total

#1: Realistic Career Vector

Section Two: Occupations that Might Appeal to You

Check the box next to any occupation or occupational grouping that interests you. Don't be concerned about having the skills or experience required, only whether the occupation appeals to you.

• If some but not all of the occupations in one group interest you, check the box and underline the particular occupations that appeal.

1. Medical Equipment Repairer
   Biomedical Equipment Technician
   X-ray Equipment Repair Specialist	

2. Wildlife Control Agent/Fish and Game Warden
   Parks and Recreation Specialist/National Park Service Ranger
   Forest and Conservation Technician/Wildlife Conservationist	

3. Building Superintendent/Facilities Manager
   Independent Home Remodeling/Improvement/Renovation Contractor
   General Building/Home Construction Contractor	

4. Police Officer/Military Officer
   Fire Inspector and Investigator
   Firefighter	

5. Radiologic (X-ray) Technologist/MRI/Radiation Therapy Technologist
   Anesthesiologist Assistant/Surgical Technologist
   Cardiovascular Technologist	

6. Emergency Medical Technician (EMT)
   Veterinary Technologist/Technician/Assistant
   Dental or Opthalmic Laboratory Technician	

(continued on next page)

(continued from previous page)

7. Farmer/Rancher/Organic Farm Manager Nursery/Greenhouse Manager Forester/Tree Surgeon	
8. Industrial Arts Teacher/Vocational Education Teacher Career and Technical Education Teacher Community College Engineering Technology Instructor	
9. Orthotist Prosthetist Optician	
10. Airplane/Commercial Pilot/Flight Engineer Aircraft Mechanic and Avionics Equipment Technician Aerospace Engineering Technician	
11. Solar Energy Systems Designer/Energy Conservation Representative Environmental Engineering Technician Environmental Protection Specialist	
12. Plant/Manufacturing Engineer/Materials Engineer Mechanical Engineer/Mechanical Engineering Technologist Tool and Die Maker/Tool Designer/Machinist	
13. Computer Systems Hardware Engineer Computer User Support Specialist Electronics Engineer	
14. Automotive Engineer Telecommunications Engineering Specialist Petroleum Engineer/Petroleum Geologist/Mining Specialist	
15. Broadcast and Sound Engineering Technician Electrical and Electronic Engineering Technologist/Technician Electro-mechanical Technician	

Total

CareerVectors

Section Three: Skills, Both Current and Potential

We will be identifying both your current motivated skills (Areas of Effectiveness) and your potential skills (Skill Areas Reflecting a Potential for Development.)

Current Motivated Skills

Please *check the box* next to any skills cluster that contains a skill that you enjoy using, gain satisfaction from, and believe you can currently perform at least reasonably well.

Potential Skills

Please review the list of skills once more. This time, note if there are any skills listed that you have not had experience using, and do not currently possess but would like to develop, think you would enjoy using, and believe you could learn to perform at least reasonably well.

Note these skills by *putting a D in the box* next to any cluster of skills that contains a skill that you would like to develop according to the guidelines above, and underline the relevant skills.

IMPORTANT NOTES

Note that often each box contains a group or cluster of related skills. You need not possess them all. If you believe that any of the skills listed apply to you, please check the box and underline the relevant skills.

As you rate your skills, try not to be overly perfectionistic or think in all or nothing terms. Give yourself the benefit of the doubt if you are not sure.

It is possible to have checks and D's in the same cluster of skills. This would indicate that you believe certain skills within that cluster apply to you now, and that there are others within the same group of skills that you would like to develop.

1. Mechanically inclined: possess mechanical/technical skills and competencies. Can fix and repair things. Skilled in using tools, machines, and mechanical equipment.	
2. Construction/building/infrastructure development skills (e.g. roads, bridges, and tunnels). Can build houses, construct buildings and other large construction projects Home improvement, renovation, and remodeling skills.	
3. Facilities management skills: can provide for the overall upkeep, maintenance, and repair of buildings.	
4. Can diagnose, troubleshoot, and solve mechanical and technical problems. Can service, maintain, fix and repair technical and mechanical equipment, home appliances, machines, and systems.	
5. Computer user/ technical support skills.	
6. Ability to work with my hands. Good physical skills and eye-hand coordination, manual dexterity, and motor skills.	

(continued on next page)

(continued from previous page)

7. Can train and care for animals. Veterinary assistant skills.	
8. Nursery/horticultural skills: can grow and care for plants and flowers. Agricultural skills: farming and ranching skills. Forestry skills.	
9. Plant operations/industrial production and manufacturing skills. Warehousing skills: knowledge of warehousing operations.	
10. Can provide protective services: law enforcement, public safety, fire fighting, and security skills.	
11. Radiologic technology skills: can administer x-rays, CT scans, and MRI exams.	
12. Can teach career and technical education courses (e.g. can teach industrial arts, engineering technology, and/or computer repair.)	
13. Engineering technology and technician skills — for example, possess mechanical engineering technology skills — can set up and operate precision machinery and tools to make high quality industrial products.	
14. Electrical/electro-mechanical/electronic technology skills; for example, can inspect, test, adjust, and repair computer and/or bio-medical equipment.	
15. Aviation skills: can pilot, navigate and repair aircraft and avionics equipment.	

SCORING INSTRUCTIONS

Total

When scoring, please do not count each box more than once. If there is a check and a (D) in the same box, please count only the one that gives you the most satisfaction.

To obtain your total score, please add up the number of boxes that contain a mark (either a check mark or a D mark) and enter your total.

Section Four: Work-Related Personality/Style Characteristics

Place a check next to any work-related personality pattern that fits with your perception of yourself. Note that not all of the traits have to apply, as long as you believe that some essential traits describe you reasonably well.

Next underline those characteristics that you believe fit you best.

1. I generally prefer to work with things and physical objects rather than with people, data, or ideas.	
2. I may have some difficulty expressing myself in words or in communicating my feelings. I am more at ease doing rather than talking.	
3. I tend to be a quite grounded, realistic, and pragmatic type of person and like to see tangible and visible results from my efforts such as a finished product.	
4. Social and interpersonal skills may not come easily to me. I may need to work on being more sensitive to the needs and feelings of others.	
5. I consider myself conservative and traditional in values and outlook. I place a high value on security and tend not to be a risk-taker. I tend to prefer a stable and predictable work environment.	
6. I am an action-oriented type of person and tend to learn best by doing and from direct, hands-on experience.	
7. I prefer to take a concrete approach to solving problems rather than an abstract or conceptual approach. I focus on what is real, concrete, and specific rather than on the possibilities and what might be.	
8. I may be too set in my ways and not as flexible as a situation may require.	
9. I am a here-and-now, present-oriented, and concrete type of person and tend not to have a future-oriented, long-range, or big picture perspective. I can see situations in black and white, and can often miss the shades of grey.	
10. I would describe myself as a practical, reliable, down-to-earth, task-oriented, and straightforward type of person. I value what is useful, sensible, and has practical utility and application.	
11. I tend not to trust hunches and intuition and instead prefer to trust practical common sense and experience in dealing with life and its problems.	
12. I tend not to be very creative, imaginative, or innovative. I would rather produce with my hands than create with my mind.	

(continued on next page)

(continued from previous page)

13. I prefer to work on tasks that are practical, tangible, structured and well defined in nature as opposed to those that are abstract, ambiguous, and open-ended. I have a low tolerance for ambiguity and like to have a structure and clear guidelines for doing things and solving problems.	
14. I tend to be somewhat shy and reserved and try to avoid situations that require me to be the center of attention.	
15. I tend not to be a highly introspective, reflective, or psychologically minded type of person.	

Total ☐

Realistic Careers: Summary Results

Compile your Realistic Career Vector totals from the previous sections.

Vector #1: Realistic Careers	Section One: General Career-Related Interests and Preferences	Section Two: Occupations that Might Appeal to You	Section Three: Skills, Both Current and Potential	Section Four: Work-Related Personality/ Style Characteristics
Totals				

#2: Investigative Career Vector

Section One: General Career-Related Interests and Preferences

Please review the clusters of career-related interests and preferences below. Check the box provided if any of the interest activity statements appeal to you.

- If some but not all of the activities mentioned within each box interest you, check the box and underline the particular activities that appeal.

- Don't hold back just because you don't believe you have the skills, education or training needed to perform the activity. If the appeal is there, check the box. Even if you have never performed the activity, if you think you would enjoy it, check the box.

1. I am interested in the life sciences (e.g. biology, genetics) the physical sciences (chemistry, physics) and the medical/health sciences.	
2. I have an interest in the behavioral and social sciences including psychology, anthropology, sociology, economics, and political science. I would enjoy conducting research in order to study and better understand social, economic, political and human behavior.	
3. For example, I would enjoy doing research on online dating behavior and the prediction of relationship compatibility and success.	
4. I am fascinated by technology and systems-related work and have a strong interest in the field of information technology (IT) and information systems. I would like to use IT to solve business and professional problems.	
5. I would get satisfaction from examining, diagnosing, and treating patients for physical, medical, and health-related conditions.	
6. I have an interest in encouraging young people (especially women and minority students) to pursue careers in science, technology, engineering, mathematics (STEM related fields). I would like to teach math and science at the high school or college level.	
7. I enjoy reading about how the body works, medicine, nutrition, health, and new developments in the treatment of disease.	
8. I would like to plan and conduct scientific and/or medical research, investigation, and experimentation. For example, I would like to study and do research on DNA and the genetic inheritance of human traits.	
9. I am interested in using analytical and quantitative skills and abilities and like using computer science, mathematical methods, and/or statistical techniques to analyze and solve problems.	
10. I would be interested in conducting economic and labor market research to assess labor market conditions and the future job outlook of various careers and professions.	

(continued on next page)

(continued from previous page)

11. I have an interest in environmental issues such as: energy conservation, air, water, noise pollution and control, solar energy and global climate change (global warming).	
12. I enjoy the study of biochemistry and biology related topics such as genetic engineering, microbiology, and molecular biology and would be interested in exploring careers in applied research, drug development, and pharmaceutical research.	
13. I am interested in biomedical engineering and would find satisfaction in the design and development of medical devices like artificial hearts and pacemakers.	
14. I like analyzing and diagnosing problems and using my intellect and expertise to find solutions to problems.	
15. I have an interest in neuroscience and the biological basis of behavior and would like to study and understand how brain functions affect human behavior.	

Total

#2: Investigative Career Vector

Section Two: Occupations that Might Appeal to You

Check the box next to any occupation or occupational grouping that interests you. Don't be concerned about having the skills or experience required, only whether the occupation appeals to you.

• If some but not all of the occupations in one group interest you, check the box and underline the particular occupations that appeal.

1. Mathematician/Operations Research Analyst Epidemiologist/Biostatistician Quantitative Finance Specialist/Actuarial Science Specialist	
2. Network Engineer/Computer Network Architect/Web Developer Medical IT/Health/Bio Informatics Specialist Forensic Computer Specialist	
3. Exercise Physiologist Public Health Service Officer/Industrial Hygienist Occupational Health and Safety Specialist	
4. Molecular Biologist/Microbiologist Marine Biologist/Oceanographer Geologist/Meteorologist	

(continued on next page)

(continued from previous page)

5. Physician/Surgeon/Dentist Physician Assistant/Nurse Practitioner/Nurse Anesthetist Veterinarian/Animal scientist	
6. Optometrist/Podiatrist/Chiropractor Pharmacist/Pharmacologist Audiologist (hearing specialist)	
7. Biologist/Geneticist/Physiologist Chemist/Biochemist Physicist/Biophysicist/Astronomer	
8. Software Developer/Engineer/Computer Programmer Computer Systems Analyst/Internet (IT) Consultant Network and Computer Systems Administrator	
9. Biomedical Researcher/Medical Scientist High School/College Math/Science Teacher STEM (Science, Technology, Engineering, Math) Educational Consultant	
10. Economist/Market Research Analyst International Economic Development Specialist Survey Researcher/Public/Political Opinion/Polling Specialist	
11. Chemical Engineer/Nuclear Engineer Civil Engineer/ Electrical Engineer Biomedical Engineer/Biochemical Engineer	
12. Experimental Psychologist/Educational Psychologist Sociologist/Anthropologist/Medical Anthropologist Archeologist/Geographer	
13. Environmental Engineer/Analyst/Consultant Environmental Sustainability Specialist/Pollution Control Engineer Climate Change Analyst	
14. Psychiatrist/Psychopharmacologist Neuroscientist/Neuropsychologist Biopsychology and Behavioral Neuroscience Specialist	
15. Biotechnology Specialist/Researcher/Consultant Medical and Clinical Laboratory Technologist/Cytotechnologist Crime Laboratory Analyst/Forensic Science Specialist/Consultant	

Total

Section Three: Skills, Both Current and Potential

We will be identifying both your current motivated skills (Areas of Effectiveness) and your potential skills (Skill Areas Reflecting a Potential for Development.)

Current Motivated Skills
Please *check the box* next to any skills cluster that contains a skill that you enjoy using, gain satisfaction from, and believe you can currently perform at least reasonably well.

Potential Skills
Please review the list of skills once more. This time, note if there are any skills listed that you have not had experience using, and do not currently possess but would like to develop, think you would enjoy using, and believe you could learn to perform at least reasonably well.

Note these skills by *putting a D in the box* next to any cluster of skills that contains a skill that you would like to develop according to the guidelines above, and underline the relevant skills.

IMPORTANT NOTES

Note that often each box contains a group or cluster of related skills. You need not possess them all. If you believe that any of the skills listed apply to you, please check the box and underline the relevant skills.

As you rate your skills, try not to be overly perfectionistic or think in all or nothing terms. Give yourself the benefit of the doubt if you are not sure.

It is possible to have checks and D's in the same cluster of skills. This would indicate that you believe certain skills within that cluster apply to you now, and that there are others within the same group of skills that you would like to develop.

1. Possess a strong grasp of scientific principles, methods, and techniques.	
2. General scientific research and investigation skills: possess research design, research methodology, data and statistical analysis skills. Possess specialized research skills including medical research and development skills, and/or biomedical, public health, and epidemiological research and analysis skills.	
3. Possess psychological and behavioral/social science research and analysis skills: can analyze, investigate, and conduct research to understand social, economic, political, and human behavior. Can diagnose psychological and/or social science and economic problems.	
4. Ability to use applied social science statistics and measurement techniques to become a knowledgeable consumer of research in education and psychology.	
5. Economic research skills: can collect, analyze, and interpret economic data. Market research/survey research and analysis skills. Public/political opinion/polling skills.	
6. Can make effective use of technology: possess good information systems and information technology (IT) skills.	

(continued on next page)

CareerVectors

7. Can use technology and IT systems to further business, professional, and organizational goals.	
8. Specialized IT skills including: Software design and development skills/computer programming skills Network engineering skills/computer network architect skills/web development skills Network and computer systems administration skills Forensic computer skills Medical computer science and health IT skills — bio informatics skills — can develop computer-based electronic health record systems.	
9. Knowledgeable regarding environmental science concepts, methods, and techniques including state-of-the art energy management programs. Can develop solutions to environmental problems.	
10. Ability to abstract, conceptualize, analyze, and solve problems. Possess inductive reasoning and critical thinking skills. Can design and develop conceptual systems and models.	
11. Possess logical and mathematical intelligence: have a strong grasp of mathematical, computer science, and statistical analysis and reasoning skills. Ability to reason with, analyze, and draw conclusions from quantitative data: can use mathematical, quantitative thinking, and statistical skills to analyze and solve problems.	
12. STEM (Science, Technology, Engineering, Mathematics) skills. For example, engineering skills: can apply a knowledge of biomedical engineering to the design, development, and evaluation of biomedical equipment, products, and devices.	
13. Can teach math and science at a high school or college level.	
14. Medical/scientific and technical writing skills (e.g. writing scientific reports, journal articles, and technical manuals).	
15. Can evaluate, diagnose, and treat people's health and medical problems. Possess medical diagnostic skills: can use state of the art diagnostic medical technology and clinical laboratory technology skills.	

SCORING INSTRUCTIONS

Total [ ]

When scoring, please do not count each box more than once. If there is a check and a (D) in the same box, please count only the one that gives you the most satisfaction.

To obtain your total score, please add up the number of boxes that contain a mark (either a check mark or a D mark) and enter your total.

Section Four: Work-Related Personality/Style Characteristics

Place a check next to any work-related personality pattern that fits with your perception of yourself. Note that not all of the traits have to apply, as long as you believe that some essential traits describe you reasonably well.

Next underline those characteristics that you believe fit you best.

1. I have a broad range of interests and tend to be a cerebral, analytical, and intellectually-oriented type of person.	
2. I am a big picture, intuitive thinker, and tend to focus on the conceptual, abstract, big picture and theoretical issues rather than on the practical, down-to-earth, and applied ones.	
3. I solve problems by thinking them through in a logical, rational, and objective manner. I tend to have a cognitive approach to life and take an impersonal, analytical, thinking, and intellectual approach to most problems and situations.	
4. I seldom allow my feelings and emotions to influence my thinking, decision-making, or judgment.	
5. For me, knowledge is power and my driving force is a quest for competence, knowledge, expertise and understanding.	
6. I can spend too much time thinking, analyzing, researching, and conceptualizing, and not enough time doing and taking practical action.	
7. I am energized by concepts and ideas and need intellectual stimulation to feel fully engaged in my work. My work needs to challenge my mind in order to keep me interested. I can get impatient with routine detail.	
8. I have a natural intellectual curiosity, an inquisitive nature, and a thoughtful, reflective and analytical mind. I am comfortable with ambiguity and cognitive complexity and enjoy tackling complex problems.	
9. I can be somewhat introverted and reserved and may be perceived, at times, as distant, aloof, and impersonal. I can also be seen as somewhat arrogant, detached, and in a world of my own.	
10. I am usually flexible and open-minded, but at times can be stubborn and controlling.	
11. I can be perfectionistic and can have unrealistically high standards and excessive expectations for myself. I can be very demanding and critical of both myself and others and can expect too much. Lack of patience can be a major problem for me.	

(continued on next page)

(continued from previous page)

12. I can over-analyze things and can be too obsessive in my thinking. My compulsiveness, perfectionism, need for thoroughness and strong desire to achieve quality standards can lead me to do excessive preparation, research and information gathering which can slow me down and interfere with my overall productivity.	
13. I have a strong need for autonomy and independence and like to experiment with new ideas, methods, and approaches. I need to work in a flexible environment and would be very frustrated in a highly structured job where very little freedom and latitude is permitted.	
14. I am frequently so task-oriented and single-minded in my drive to accomplish a goal that I may overlook the human element and may not realize the impact of my behavior on others.	
15. I can have an imbalanced profile: strong technically and conceptually, but weak interpersonally. I may need to work on being more aware, sensitive, and responsive to the feelings, needs, and concerns of others.	

Total ☐

Investigative Careers: Summary Results

Compile your Investigative Career Vector totals from the previous sections.

Vector #2: Investigative Careers	Section One: General Career-Related Interests and Preferences	Section Two: Occupations that Might Appeal to You	Section Three: Skills, Both Current and Potential	Section Four: Work-Related Personality/ Style Characteristics
Totals				

#3: Artistic Career Vector

Section One: General Career-Related Interests and Preferences

Please review the clusters of career-related interests and preferences below. Check the box provided if any of the interest activity statements appeal to you.

- If some but not all of the activities mentioned within each box interest you, check the box and underline the particular activities that appeal.

- Don't hold back just because you don't believe you have the skills, education or training needed to perform the activity. If the appeal is there, check the box. Even if you have never performed the activity, if you think you would enjoy it, check the box.

1. I have an interest in artistic activities and occupations that provide outlets for my creativity and opportunities for self-expression. I enjoy expressing my thoughts and feelings creatively through various artistic media.	
2. I like doing creative handcrafts such as ceramics, needlepoint, jewelry making, weaving, and making quilts.	
3. I enjoy expressing my creativity in various ways including designing and developing new programs, products, and services, and creating new ideas, possibilities, and innovative approaches to problems.	
4. I have an interest in the culinary arts and enjoy catering activities, gourmet cooking, and eating in gourmet restaurants.	
5. I like writing and journalistic activities. I would like to write for online media including blogs, social media websites, and electronic newsletters.	
6. I enjoy creative activities and functions including imagining, inventing, visualizing, brainstorming, divergent thinking, the use of intuitive abilities, and seeing things from a different perspective.	
7. I enjoy the performing arts, music, dance, film, drama, and the theater.	
8. I like performing, acting, singing, dancing, and/or playing a musical instrument. I would also like to write songs, produce music, and record it digitally.	
9. I have an interest in the field of digital multimedia design and would enjoy creating computer-generated visual images, animation, and special effects for movies/TV and entertainment products such as computer games and music videos.	
10. I would like to teach art appreciation on an elementary or high school level. On a college level, I would like to teach subjects such as art history, film and media studies, and/or courses in design and the visual arts.	

(continued on next page)

(continued from previous page)

11. I would enjoy being an architect and planning and designing buildings. I would also enjoy helping people decorate their homes and offices and meet their interior design needs.	
12. I would like to write, edit, act in, direct, and/or produce movies, film, and TV programs.	
13. I would like to manage an arts organization such as a performing arts center, an art gallery, museum, or theater. I would also like to start and manage an online art related business.	
14. I would like to design and build a creative website. I would also like to design an app for mobile devices.	
15. I would like to be photojournalist and take quality pictures using state-of-the-art digital photography.	

Total

#3: Artistic Career Vector

Section Two: Occupations that Might Appeal to You

Check the box next to any occupation or occupational grouping that interests you. Don't be concerned about having the skills or experience required, only whether the occupation appeals to you.

- If some but not all of the occupations in one group interest you, check the box and underline the particular occupations that appeal.

1. Photographer/Photojournalist Medical/Scientific Illustrator Fashion Illustrator	
2. Journalist/Reporter Radio/TV Broadcaster/Announcer/News Anchor News/Sports/Weather Director	
3. Interior Designer/Fashion Designer/Graphic Designer Web/App Designer Industrial Designer/Product Designer	
4. Film Maker/Film Producer/Film Director Film/Video Editor Actor/Drama Coach/Casting Director	

(continued on next page)

(continued from previous page)

5. Creative Arts Therapist (Art, Music, Dance, Drama Therapist) Museum Education Director Educational Theater Specialist	
6. Architect Landscape Architect Garden Designer/Environmental Designer	
7. Book/Magazine Publisher Digital Publishing Specialist Book/Magazine/Newspaper Editor	
8. Corporate Communications Specialist/Media Consultant Public Relations Specialist/Advertising Account Executive/Copywriter Digital Communications and Media Specialist/Social Media Producer	
9. Digital Multimedia Design and Production Specialist Game Design and Development Specialist/Computer Video Game Designer Multimedia Artist and Animator	
10. Musician/Music Director/Composer/Arranger Songwriter/Record/Music Producer Entertainer/Performer/Singer/Dancer	
11. Art Appraiser/Art Restoration Specialist Art/Antique Dealer Graphic Arts Sales Representative	
12. Blogger/Online Content Developer Writer of Fiction/Nonfiction TV/Documentary/Film/Screenwriter	
13. Arts Organization Administrator/Museum/Art Gallery Director Corporate Art Consultant Art Director	
14. Gourmet Catering Specialist Culinary Arts Specialist Owner/Operator of a Professional Catering Business	
15. Art/Music/Drama Teacher/Art Librarian English/Foreign Language Teacher Professor of Film/Media Studies/Art History	

Total

Section Three: Skills, Both Current and Potential

We will be identifying both your current motivated skills (Areas of Effectiveness) and your potential skills (Skill Areas Reflecting a Potential for Development.)

Current Motivated Skills

Please *check the box* next to any skills cluster that contains a skill that you enjoy using, gain satisfaction from, and believe you can currently perform at least reasonably well.

Potential Skills

Please review the list of skills once more. This time, note if there are any skills listed that you have not had experience using, and do not currently possess but would like to develop, think you would enjoy using, and believe you could learn to perform at least reasonably well.

Note these skills by *putting a D in the box* next to any cluster of skills that contains a skill that you would like to develop according to the guidelines above, and underline the relevant skills.

IMPORTANT NOTES

Note that often each box contains a group or cluster of related skills. You need not possess them all. If you believe that any of the skills listed apply to you, please check the box and underline the relevant skills.

As you rate your skills, try not to be overly perfectionistic or think in all or nothing terms. Give yourself the benefit of the doubt if you are not sure.

It is possible to have checks and D's in the same cluster of skills. This would indicate that you believe certain skills within that cluster apply to you now, and that there are others within the same group of skills that you would like to develop.

1. Can understand and apply artistic principles and techniques. Can creatively express myself and convey thoughts/ideas and feelings through an artistic medium.	
2. Ability to think visually and possess a strong sense of color, design, shape and texture. Visual and spatial perception skills: can work with spatial concepts as in interior design and architecture.	
3. Performing arts skills: can act, sing, dance, perform, and/or entertain others. Musical knowledge and skills: can read, compose music, and/or play a musical instrument. Can write songs, produce music, and record it digitally.	
4. Good writing, editing, and journalism skills. Possess writing skills for online media such as websites, blogs, social media, and electronic newsletters. Strong language skills: can learn and speak a foreign language.	
5. Digital communications and media skills. Digital advertising and publishing skills.	

(continued on next page)

6. Public relations and corporate communication skills. Can create effective advertising promotion ideas and write advertising copy. Good business writing skills.	
7. Gourmet cooking and catering skills. Can teach culinary arts and/or be a professional food critic.	
8. Design skills (e.g. graphic design, industrial design, set design, jewelry design, fashion design and digital design) Web design skills: can design and build a creative website and/or an app for mobile devices.	
9. Digital art skills: digital and multimedia art, design, and production skills. Can use computer design software to create visual images, animation, and visual effects for film and television. Game design and development skills: can create entertainment products such as computer games and music videos.	
10. Photography skills: can take quality photographs and possess a knowledge of digital photography software.	
11. Can act, write, direct, and/or produce films, plays, and TV programs. Possess film and video editing skills.	
12. Creative art therapy skills: art, music, dance and drama therapy skills.	
13. Arts administration and management skills: including a knowledge of relevant art appraisal, marketing, (including internet and social media marketing,) managerial, fundraising, legal, financial, and technology skills. Can manage arts organizations such as museums, art galleries, theaters and online art businesses.	
14. Art education skills. Can teach art at the elementary, high school, and/or college level. Skills in teaching English/foreign languages.	
15. Intuitive abilities: can use intuition to identify issues, solve problems, make decisions, and help gain insight into and understand others. Capacity for divergent and innovative thinking.	

SCORING INSTRUCTIONS   Total

*When scoring, please do not count each box more than once. If there is a check and a (D)
in the same box, please count only the one that gives you the most satisfaction.*

*To obtain your total score, please add up the number of boxes that contain a mark
(either a check mark or a D mark) and enter your total.*

Section Four: Work-Related Personality/Style Characteristics

Place a check next to any work-related personality pattern that fits with your perception of yourself. Note that not all of the traits have to apply, as long as you believe that some essential traits describe you reasonably well.

Next underline those characteristics that you believe fit you best.

1. I am flexible and adaptable. I can adapt well to change and can modify my approach as the situation requires.	
2. I may have difficulty dealing with routine details, non-meaningful tasks, and the often tedious, practical requirements of daily life such as balancing my checkbook and paying my bills on time.	
3. I tend to have difficulty getting and keeping organized, and dealing with tasks and activities that require a high degree of organization, structure, and attention to detail.	
4. I have a strong need for independence, autonomy, latitude and freedom in the way I do things. I work best in a flexible environment where I don't feel restricted by excessive rules, regulations, structure and bureaucracy.	
5. I show an openness to experience and am willing to take risks and try new and unfamiliar activities such as travel to a foreign country for the first time.	
6. I can have problems with setting priorities and difficulty making decisions and commitments. I can, at times, be somewhat impractical and not especially realistic and pragmatic.	
7. My personality make-up includes a strong need for change, flexibility, creativity, novelty, and self-expression. I can become bored easily with too much routine, repetition, and lack of creative challenge.	
8. I am comfortable with ambiguity, uncertainty, lack of structure and open-ended situations.	
9. I like to "go with the flow," and tend to deal with life in an open-ended, flexible and spontaneous manner rather than in a planned, organized, structured, and controlled way. I tend to be a "fly by the seat of my pants" kind of person and like keeping my options open and not being tied down.	
10. I can act impulsively and "on the spur of the moment." I may tend to "wing it," and may not think things through sufficiently, consider the consequences, or plan and prepare enough before taking action.	
11. My failure to manage my time well can often result in my feeling overwhelmed, tense, anxious, and disorganized.	

(continued on next page)

(continued from previous page)

12. My work habits can be erratic, inconsistent, and uneven depending on my mood and how much interest I have in what I am doing. When I lose interest, I can have difficulty applying myself.	
13. Procrastination has been a frequent problem for me. I can postpone unpleasant tasks that need to be done and can procrastinate on activities I find uninteresting, anxiety provoking, frustrating, and/or difficult.	
14. I often have difficulty completing projects. I have a tendency to start many things, jump from one thing to another, and often not finish what I start.	
15. I am sensitive and emotional by nature and make use of my feelings and intuition as guides to problem solving and decision-making.	

Total

Artistic Careers: Summary Results

Compile your Artistic Career Vector totals from the previous sections.

#3: Artistic Career Vector	Section One: General Career-Related Interests and Preferences	Section Two: Occupations that Might Appeal to You	Section Three: Skills, Both Current and Potential	Section Four: Work-Related Personality/ Style Characteristics
Totals				

#4: Social Career Vector

Section One: General Career-Related Interests and Preferences

Please review the clusters of career-related interests and preferences below. Check the box provided if any of the interest activity statements appeal to you.

- If some but not all of the activities mentioned within each box interest you, check the box and underline the particular activities that appeal.

- Don't hold back just because you don't believe you have the skills, education or training needed to perform the activity. If the appeal is there, check the box. Even if you have never performed the activity, if you think you would enjoy it, check the box.

1. I would gain satisfaction from helping people to improve their eating habits, modify negative eating behaviors, and select healthy foods to enhance their overall physical health and well being.	
2. I would find it satisfying to work as a mental health professional. I have an interest in helping people deal with mental health issues and emotional and psychological problems such as anxiety, depression, and low self-esteem.	
3. I would like to help individuals to enhance their relationships with others by assisting them to develop and/or improve their emotional intelligence, empathy, and interpersonal sensitivity/effectiveness.	
4. I would like to work for a college/university Office of Career Development and assist college students to choose college majors, establish career goals, develop effective job search skills, and obtain internships and jobs.	
5. I get satisfaction from helping others learn and enjoy teaching, tutoring, training, and educational activities.	
6. I have an interest in the psychology of personality and understanding individual differences in people including their personality characteristics, styles of functioning, and psychological type and temperament.	
7. I like helping people to understand themselves better, gain insight into their core strengths and weaknesses, and make good choices and decisions.	
8. I find satisfaction in helping others and enjoy guiding, coaching, and mentoring others and facilitating self-exploration and self-development. I like helping people to develop their potential and improve their professional effectiveness.	
9. I get satisfaction from treating, healing, nursing, and improving the overall health and wellness of people.	
10. I get satisfaction from helping people with disabilities and providing them with special education, disability and rehabilitation services. For example, I would like to provide counseling and academic support services for college students with learning disabilities and/or attention deficit disorders.	

(continued on next page)

(continued from previous page)

11. I am interested in helping people to modify and/or change negative health habits and behaviors such as binge eating, smoking, problem drinking, internet addiction, and substance abuse including addiction to prescription painkillers.	
12. I have an interest in working with and helping children, the disabled, and/or the elderly.	
13. I gain satisfaction from counseling others. I like assisting people with their personal problems and concerns by talking, exploring feelings, and helping them to develop effective strategies to deal with their problems.	
14. I am drawn to opportunities to provide practical services for people. I like informing and advising others and providing practical information and support to aid in planning and decision-making. I would enjoy working in a college/university academic advisement center or career information resource center.	
15. I am interested in the field of social work and would like to help people cope with challenges in their lives such as divorce, unemployment, family problems and major illness.	

Total [ ]

#4: Social Career Vector

Section Two: Occupations that Might Appeal to You

Check the box next to any occupation or occupational grouping that interests you. Don't be concerned about having the skills or experience required, only whether the occupation appeals to you.

• If some but not all of the occupations in one group interest you, check the box and underline the particular occupations that appeal.

1. College Academic Advisor/Admissions Counselor/International Student Advisor Counselor in a College Counseling Center/Student Development Center Counselor in a College Office of Disabilities Services	
2. Elementary/High School Teacher/School Principal Librarian/School/College Librarian/School Counselor ESL/Bilingual and Multicultural Education Specialist	
3. Career Counselor/Career Development Specialist/Career Coach Counselor in a College Career Services Office Career Transition/Retirement Counseling Specialist	

(continued on next page)

(continued from previous page)

4. Psychotherapist/Clinical Social Worker/Eating Disorders Specialist Marriage, Family, and Child Therapist/Sex Therapist Cognitive Behavioral Therapist	
5. Speech Therapist/Speech Language Pathologist/Recreational Therapist Occupational Therapist/Physical Therapist Community Health Educator	
6. Registered Nurse/Clinical Nurse Specialist/Psychiatric Nurse Clinical Dietician/Certified Diabetes Educator Dental Hygienist	
7. Mental Health Counselor/Alcohol and Substance Abuse Counselor Counselor in an Inpatient/Outpatient Drug Treatment Program Vocational Rehab Counselor/Psychiatric Rehabilitation Specialist	
8. Reading and Learning Disabilities Specialist/Consultant Special Education Teacher/Consultant Advocate for People with Disabilities/Hearing Loss Specialist	
9. Minister/Priest/Rabbi/Pastoral Counselor Director of Religious Education Synagogue/Church Youth Director	
10. Counseling Psychologist/School Psychologist/Clinical Psychologist Clinical Health Psychologist/Clinical Neuropsychologist Psychological Evaluation Specialist	
11. Probation/Parole Officer Criminal Justice Specialist/Applied Criminologist Forensic Psychologist	
12. Director of a Supported Housing Program for Disabled Individuals Director of Children and Family Services for a Social Work Agency Director of Foster Care and Adoption Services	
13. ADD/ADHD Coach/Health/Wellness Coach Social Skills/Relationship/Emotional Intelligence Coach/Consultant Life Coach	
14. LGBT Service Coordinator/Director of Volunteer Services Social Worker/School/Medical Social Worker Community Organizer/Community Relations Specialist	
15. Clinical Gerontologist/Geriatric Social Worker Professional Geriatric Care Manager Adult Development and Aging Specialist	

Total

Section Three: Skills, Both Current and Potential

We will be identifying both your current motivated skills (Areas of Effectiveness) and your potential skills (Skill Areas Reflecting a Potential for Development.)

Current Motivated Skills
Please *check the box* next to any skills cluster that contains a skill that you enjoy using, gain satisfaction from, and believe you can currently perform at least reasonably well.

Potential Skills
Please review the list of skills once more. This time, note if there are any skills listed that you have not had experience using, and do not currently possess but would like to develop, think you would enjoy using, and believe you could learn to perform at least reasonably well.

Note these skills by *putting a D in the box* next to any cluster of skills that contains a skill that you would like to develop according to the guidelines above, and underline the relevant skills.

IMPORTANT NOTES

Note that often each box contains a group or cluster of related skills. You need not possess them all. If you believe that any of the skills listed apply to you, please check the box and underline the relevant skills.

As you rate your skills, try not to be overly perfectionistic or think in all or nothing terms. Give yourself the benefit of the doubt if you are not sure.

It is possible to have checks and D's in the same cluster of skills. This would indicate that you believe certain skills within that cluster apply to you now, and that there are others within the same group of skills that you would like to develop.

1. Social, interpersonal, and relationship building skills: the ability to connect with others and develop and maintain harmonious working relationships. Group facilitation skills: can lead and facilitate small groups. Can develop and conduct support groups for individuals with special needs such as recently divorced individuals.	
2. General counseling skills: Effective at helping people with personal problems Can help others to explore and understand themselves, make suitable choices and decisions, and effectively cope with their problems and difficulties Can design and develop effective counseling and behavioral change interventions	
3. Specialized counseling skills including: Marital/relationship counseling skills (including pre-marital counseling, family counseling, counseling for sexual difficulties and divorce mediation) Vocational rehabilitation counseling skills Alcoholism and substance abuse counseling and treatment skills Mental health counseling skills School/college counseling skills Bereavement counseling skills Program development/program evaluation skills	

(continued on next page)

(continued from previous page)

4. Assessment and self-exploration skills: can facilitate self-exploration and self-development.

   Can help individuals to identify, understand, and articulate their strengths and weaknesses and their interests, values, and personality characteristics.

   Can use assessment instruments and techniques to help individuals to understand themselves.

5. Effective at mentoring, coaching, and developing others.

   Can help others to capitalize on their strengths and manage their weaknesses and development needs.

6. Informing/advising/academic advising skills: can provide helpful information to aid in decision-making.

7. Educational skills: can help others learn. Teaching, instructing, tutoring and training skills.

   Can identify the educational needs and learning styles of students, and conduct effective educational programs.

   Possess specialized educational skills including curriculum development skills, teaching ESL, bilingual and multicultural education skills, special education skills and the ability to use technology as a teaching/learning/training tool.

8. Interviewing skills: can put people at ease, draw people out, and effectively obtain information from others.

   Active listening skills/ability to really listen to people and try to understand their problems.

9. Can interact and work effectively with different kinds of people including people of different cultural backgrounds.

   Possess multicultural competence: shows the awareness, knowledge, sensitivity and ability to adapt successfully and function effectively in an increasingly culturally diverse and multicultural society.

   Multicultural sensitivity and diversity skills: awareness and sensitivity to multicultural and diversity issues.

10. Interpersonal sensitivity and empathy skills: sensitive and responsive to the feelings, needs, problems, and concerns of others.

    Emotional intelligence skills including: self awareness, self-management, social awareness and relationship management skills/social skills.

    Has the ability to monitor and recognize one's own feelings, and those of others, influence others, and effectively manage one's emotions.

11. Can provide health care, medical, treatment, and rehabilitation services to facilitate, improve, and maintain the physical health and wellbeing of individuals.

    Can provide a variety of specialized health-related skills and services including:

    Nursing skills

    Physical and occupational therapy skills

    Speech therapy skills

    Infertility counseling skills/Genetic counseling skills

    Nutritional counseling skills

    Certified Diabetes educator skills

    Holistic health care skills (e.g. acupuncture and massage therapy)

    Senior health care services (e.g. assisted living and nursing home skills)

(continued on next page)

(continued from previous page)

12. Can provide psychological services to individuals (children, adolescents, adults) couples, groups, and families. Psychotherapy and mental health counseling and treatment skills: can evaluate, diagnose and treat emotional, and psychological problems such as anxiety, depression, and low self-esteem Can help individuals to modify and/or change dysfunctional behavioral patterns, maladaptive thinking/negative feelings, and internal barriers.	
13. Career counseling skills: can assist individuals to reduce career confusion, make career choices, and find vocational direction. Can also help people to make transitions (e.g. career changes and retirement) manage their careers, and provide assistance with the job search process.	
14. Social work skills: knowledge of the principles and practices of social work. Can help people cope with challenges in their lives such as divorce, unemployment, family problems, and major illness. Specialized social work and related skills including: Clinical social work skills: can provide individual, family, and couples therapy and treatment skills Possess strong diagnostic assessment skills Crisis intervention skills Geriatric social work skills Clinical gerontology skills: can treat problems related to aging and can plan and develop services to meet the needs and problems of seniors and the elderly Professional geriatric care management skills	
15. Can assist people with disabilities: can provide disability and rehabilitation services including special education services for children, adolescents, and adults with a variety of special needs. Can provide counseling, special accommodations, and academic support services for college students with learning disabilities and/or attention deficit disorders.	

Total

SCORING INSTRUCTIONS

When scoring, please do not count each box more than once. If there is a check and a (D) in the same box, please count only the one that gives you the most satisfaction.

To obtain your total score, please add up the number of boxes that contain a mark (either a check mark or a D mark) and enter your total.

Section Four: Work-Related Personality/Style Characteristics

Place a check next to any work-related personality pattern that fits with your perception of yourself. Note that not all of the traits have to apply, as long as you believe that some essential traits describe you reasonably well.

Next underline those characteristics that you believe fit you best.

1. I am friendly, value cooperation, seek harmony, and try to avoid conflict and hurting other people's feelings. To get along with others, I can be overly accommodating, deferential, agreeable, and submissive in my interactions with people.	
2. I can have difficulty being assertive, and asking others for what I need. I can also have difficulty being a self-promoter, and selling and marketing myself.	
3. I show interpersonal sensitivity, and am understanding, empathic, sensitive, and responsive to the feelings, needs, problems, and concerns of others.	
4. I have a need for affiliation (social interaction) and a strong need to be needed. I need to be heard, listened to, and understood and value support, encouragement, and understanding from others.	
5. I am able to interact and relate well to a wide variety of people including people from different multicultural backgrounds.	
6. I worry that I may be perceived as too mild-mannered, soft-hearted, and possibly not assertive, forceful, aggressive, confident, and strong enough to be considered for advancement to a managerial role.	
7. I tend to be more people and relationship-oriented than task oriented. However, this can result in my not being sufficiently results-oriented and paying enough attention to goal achievement, task-accomplishment, and getting things done.	
8. For me to be happy, my work has to be meaningful and in harmony with my core values. I have to believe in and care about what I do.	
9. I may approach life and problem-solving in a more feeling, subjective, and emotional manner rather than in a more analytical, objective, thinking, and logical fashion. I have to watch out for my tendency to permit my feelings and emotions to color my judgment.	
10. I can be overly concerned with what others think of me, especially those in a position of authority. I have a strong need for approval and external validation to feel good about myself.	

(continued on next page)

(continued from previous page)

11. I can be overly sensitive and thin-skinned at times, and can take things too personally. I can be especially sensitive to perceived criticism from others.	
12. I may need to develop a greater tough-mindedness, sense of objectivity, and a thicker skin in order to be more effective in my work and better able to deal with criticism, conflict, adversity, and stress.	
13. I have to watch out not to be overly trusting, forthright, and naïve when relating to others and not sufficiently objective and/or politically and socially astute.	
14. I have the ability to be accepting, flexible, and patient when working with others and can remain calm when working with clients including those who are distressed, frustrated, and/or angry.	
15. I am comfortable in a helping and/or influencer role such as a teacher/trainer, counselor, advisor, coach, clinician, mentor or facilitator but where pure management activities and responsibilities are limited.	

Total

Social Careers: Summary Results

Compile your Social Career Vector totals from the previous sections.

#4: Social Career Vector	Section One: General Career-Related Interests and Preferences	Section Two: Occupations that Might Appeal to You	Section Three: Skills, Both Current and Potential	Section Four: Work-Related Personality/ Style Characteristics
Totals				

#5: Enterprising Career Vector

Section One: General Career-Related Interests and Preferences

Please review the clusters of career-related interests and preferences below. Check the box provided if any of the interest activity statements appeal to you.

- If some but not all of the activities mentioned within each box interest you, check the box and underline the particular activities that appeal.

- Don't hold back just because you don't believe you have the skills, education or training needed to perform the activity. If the appeal is there, check the box. Even if you have never performed the activity, if you think you would enjoy it, check the box.

1. I have business-oriented interests and enjoy solving business problems, making business decisions and negotiating business transactions. I also enjoy tasks involving influencing and persuading others, public speaking, and selling and promoting products, ideas, and/or services.	
2. I am interested in general marketing activities such as brand management, advertising, public relations, online/internet marketing, sales, international marketing and business development activities.	
3. I am also interested in the use of digital media, e-commerce, and social media tools to help new business owners market and promote their products and services.	
4. I have entrepreneurial interests and would enjoy developing a comprehensive business plan and starting, operating and managing my own business or buying a franchise.	
5. I am interested in strategic business planning and would like to help develop the strategies, policies, and programs needed to provide the overall direction for an organization and achieve its long-term strategic goals.	
6. I would gain satisfaction from helping people and organizations with their legal problems, and providing legal services.	
7. I have an interest in finance, investments, real estate, venture capital, and the management of money and financial assets for individuals and organizations. I like to follow the stock market and invest in stocks, bonds, and/or mutual funds.	
8. I would like to assist and advise others regarding their investments, and general financial and estate planning needs.	
9. I am interested in the effective management of health care facilities and medical services and would like to manage a well-run hospital or community urgent care center.	
10. I like to read business books, magazines, and the business section of the newspaper. I also enjoy reading publications such as *The Wall Street Journal*, *Bloomberg Businessweek* and the *Harvard Business Review*.	

(continued on next page)

(continued from previous page)

11. I like to manage people, programs, and projects. I like to lead, influence, direct and manage people to achieve organizational goals and obtain economic success.	
12. I am interested in the field of human resource management and would enjoy planning, directing, coordinating and managing the human resource functions for an organization.	
13. I would like to help organizations plan and manage their computer-related activities and make maximum use of their IT resources and information systems. For example, I would like to be an IT project manager and plan, initiate and manage information technology (IT) projects for an organization.	
14. I would like to provide the employees of an organization with training, coaching, career development, mentoring, and talent management programs to help improve themselves and facilitate greater career success and satisfaction.	
15. I am interested in financial management and would like to manage, direct, and coordinate the financial resources, activities, and operations for an organization.	

Total

#5: Enterprising Career Vector

Section Two: Occupations that Might Appeal to You

Check the box next to any occupation or occupational grouping that interests you. Don't be concerned about having the skills or experience required, only whether the occupation appeals to you.

• If some but not all of the occupations in one group interest you, check the box and underline the particular occupations that appeal.

1. Executive General Manager Management Consultant/Business Consultant	
2. Financial Manager Corporate Finance Specialist/Investment Banking Professional International Finance Specialist	
3. Investment Fund/Mutual Fund/Hedge Fund Manager Investment Advisor/Financial Planner/Estate Planner Securities/Commodities/Financial Services Sales Agent	

(continued on next page)

(continued from previous page)

4. Non-profit Agency Manager/Airport Manager Medical and Health Services/Hospital/Urgent Care Center Director Corporate Fitness and Wellness Consultant	
5. Human Resources Manager/HR Generalist/HR Specialist Training and Development Manager/Diversity Manager Compensation and Benefits Manager	
6. Lawyer/Judge/Director of Legal Affairs Politician/Political Strategist/Lobbyist/Foreign Service Officer Public Policy Specialist/Urban Planner	
7. Entrepreneur/Venture Capital/Business Franchising Specialist Small Business Owner/Retail Business Manager Fashion Coordinator/Merchandise Buyer/Purchasing Agent	
8. Marketing Director/ Director of International/Global Marketing E-Commerce/Social Media/Digital Media Marketing Director/Strategist International Business/Trade Specialist/International Wine Dealer	
9. Industrial/Organizational Psychologist/Executive Coach Management and Leadership Development Specialist Organizational Behavior/Development/Change Specialist	
10. Information Technology (IT) Manager/IT Project Manager Computer and Information Systems Manager Director of Internet Services and Marketing/IT Recruiter	
11. Environmental Sustainability Manager Emergency/Disaster Management Specialist/Consultant Security Manager/Consultant/Regulatory Affairs Manager	
12. Hotel/Motel/Restaurant Manager/Chef/Food Service Manager Hospitality/Tourism/Special Events/Sports Management Specialist Funeral Director	
13. Educational Administrator/Principal/School Superintendent College and University Administrator Director of Admissions/Director of Student Affairs	
14. Real Estate Developer/Manager Real Estate Sales Agent/Broker/Mortgage Broker Real Estate Property Manager	
15. Fundraiser/Director of Development Sales/Advertising and Promotion Manager/PR Manager Business Manager/Agent for Artists, Performers, Writers, and Athletes	

Total

Section Three: Skills, Both Current and Potential

We will be identifying both your current motivated skills (Areas of Effectiveness) and your potential skills (Skill Areas Reflecting a Potential for Development.)

Current Motivated Skills

Please *check the box* next to any skills cluster that contains a skill that you enjoy using, gain satisfaction from, and believe you can currently perform at least reasonably well.

Potential Skills

Please review the list of skills once more. This time, note if there are any skills listed that you have not had experience using, and do not currently possess but would like to develop, think you would enjoy using, and believe you could learn to perform at least reasonably well.

Note these skills by *putting a D in the box* next to any cluster of skills that contains a skill that you would like to develop according to the guidelines above, and underline the relevant skills.

IMPORTANT NOTES

Note that often each box contains a group or cluster of related skills. You need not possess them all. If you believe that any of the skills listed apply to you, please check the box and underline the relevant skills.

As you rate your skills, try not to be overly perfectionistic or think in all or nothing terms. Give yourself the benefit of the doubt if you are not sure.

It is possible to have checks and D's in the same cluster of skills. This would indicate that you believe certain skills within that cluster apply to you now, and that there are others within the same group of skills that you would like to develop.

1. Strong business acumen, business judgment, decision-making and problem solving skills Strategic thinking, planning, and management skills Management/organizational consulting skills	
2. General managerial competencies and skills: can manage people, projects, and programs to attain organizational goals and/or economic success. Can supervise and direct the work of others to get things done. Can plan, manage, and control the daily functions of an organization.	
3. Specialized management skills including: Non-profit management skills Medical and health services management skills including hospital and nursing home administration skills Hospitality, hotel, tourism, special event, and sports management skills Management of educational services and programs Sustainability program management skills: can develop and implement programs to achieve energy efficiency and management for an organization.	
4. Relationship building and networking skills: can establish, build, and maintain strong client, customer and professional networks and relationships. Interpersonal effectiveness — good social/interpersonal skills — can deal effectively with people Shows emotional intelligence matched with the ability to get things done	

(continued on next page)

(continued from previous page)

5. Human resource management skills: can plan, direct, and coordinate the human resource functions for an organization.

   These include compensation and benefits, diversity management, regulatory compliance, and recruiting and staffing functions.

6. Strong business communication skills: effective verbal and written communication skills. Strong public speaking/presentation skills. Ability to make PowerPoint presentations.

   Ability to influence and persuade others. Possess good negotiation skills: can negotiate contracts, transactions, agreements, and prices.

7. Political skills and organizational awareness: knows how to maneuver within an organization to get things done. Can navigate office politics.

   Legal skills: can assist individuals and organizations with legal problems and provide legal services.

8. General marketing skills — knowledge of marketing principles and practices — can analyze the needs of the marketplace and consumer needs and develop effective marketing strategies and programs.

   Specialized marketing skills including:

   Brand development and management skills

   Healthcare marketing skills

   Technical and Pharmaceutical marketing skills

   Medical products marketing skills

   Financial services marketing skills

   Fundraising and development skills

   Buying, merchandising, and retail skills

   International trade/import/export skills

9. Can effectively use interactive digital media marketing and online marketing tools to promote and build a business.

   This includes websites, search engine marketing, e-commerce, email marketing and social media marketing skills.

10. Possess international/global marketing and business skills: ability to reach global markets including knowledge of doing business with China, India and other emerging markets.

    Possess the skills, temperament, and personal characteristics to succeed in an overseas, international (expatriate) assignment.

(continued on next page)

11. Sales, promotion, advertising and business development skills: can sell and promote ideas, products, and services. Customer service skills. Real estate sales/brokering skills, real estate development skills (e.g. building hotels, condominiums, and shopping centers) Property management skills. Mortgage brokering skills.	
12. Entrepreneurial skills: can start, build, manage, and operate a successful business venture/consulting practice. Venture capital/business franchising skills.	
13. Business application of technology: can effectively utilize current computer software and information technology systems to achieve business and professional goals. Computer and information systems management skills/information technology (IT) management skills/IT project management skills: can plan, coordinate, direct, and manage the use of computer systems and IT related activities and projects for an organization.	
14. Can provide human resource development programs and services for employees including training and development, management and leadership development, executive coaching, career development and talent management programs. Effective at coaching, mentoring, and developing others. Can assess the strengths and development needs of employees and provide useful feedback to enhance their job performance and professional effectiveness. Can help employees to manage their careers.	
15. Financial management skills: ability to manage money, finances, and investments for individuals and organizations. Can manage, direct, and coordinate all financial resources, activities, and operations for an organization. Investment advisory and financial and estate planning skills. Trading skills: can buy and sell securities (stocks, bonds, and mutual funds).	

Total

SCORING INSTRUCTIONS

When scoring, please do not count each box more than once. If there is a check and a (D) in the same box, please count only the one that gives you the most satisfaction.

To obtain your total score, please add up the number of boxes that contain a mark (either a check mark or a D mark) and enter your total.

Section Four: Work-Related Personality/Style Characteristics

Place a check next to any work-related personality pattern that fits with your perception of yourself. Note that not all of the traits have to apply, as long as you believe that some essential traits describe you reasonably well.

Next underline those characteristics that you believe fit you best.

1. I believe I have the temperament and confidence to be comfortable and effective in a position of authority, and to be able to assume a take-charge role. I am flexible and adaptable, and can project a strong sense of self and self-confidence without arrogance. I am socially adept, and have poise and self-assurance when dealing with others.	
2. I can be too task-oriented and overly concerned with getting things done and not sufficiently relationship-oriented. In order to improve my interpersonal effectiveness, I need to show more awareness and sensitivity to the feelings, needs, and concerns of others.	
3. I have a high need for control and can, at times, micromanage and not delegate well. I can lack patience with people and not take the time to really listen well. I can also lack tact and diplomacy and can, at times, be blunt and overly direct with others.	
4. I show a capacity for independent thinking and action. I can take initiative, and take a proactive, action-oriented approach rather than a passive, reactive approach to situations, problems and opportunities as they occur.	
5. I seek tangible rewards, recognition, and am motivated by economic gain. I have a strong need for achievement, dominance (power) and control. I like to feel in control and make things happen.	
6. I can make decisions in a timely manner, rather than vacillating, hesitating, procrastinating, or being indecisive. I can act quickly and decisively and have the courage to make tough decisions. I try to do what is right and not just what is politically expedient.	
7. I show the energy, persistence, perseverance, tenacity, and stick-to-it-ness necessary to achieve results. I am also ambitious, competitive, and can aggressively pursue business and professional goals and opportunities.	
8. I am goal-oriented, and have a strong results orientation and sense of urgency to produce results and get things done as quickly as possible without sacrificing quality.	
9. I possess a relatively good level of ego strength, strong stress management and coping skills, and can work well under pressure. I exhibit a strong resilience and can recover and bounce back from adversity and setbacks and not be easily discouraged. In addition, I possess the personal resources to handle difficult work situations and overcome career barriers, obstacles and challenges.	

(continued on next page)

(continued from previous page)

10. I have a realistic and accurate self-assessment. I know my management style and I know what motivates me. I also know my strengths, limitations, internal barriers, and areas in need of development. I am able to use my self-knowledge to make good choices/decisions, and to capitalize on my strengths and manage my weaknesses.	
11. I may not always be aware of my interpersonal impact and how others see me. I have been told that I can be perceived, at times, as domineering, critical, controlling, demanding, and somewhat intimidating.	
12. I can be appropriately direct, firm, tough-minded, and assertive when necessary without being abrasive. I can also confront, deal with, and handle problems, difficult people and situations in a timely manner.	
13. I have the confidence to influence and persuade others without being overbearing and can be a self-promoter and sell and market myself.	
14. I am enterprising and aggressive by nature, possess an entrepreneurial spirit, and believe I have the temperament to be effective in an entrepreneurial role. For example, I have the drive, independence, stamina, and courage required and am proactive, decisive, and willing to take prudent risks.	
15. I believe I possess the personal attributes, behavior patterns, and core competencies to work effectively in the world of competitive business. I am emotionally strong enough to handle the demands of a tough business/corporate environment and am able to work and function effectively in a fast-paced, highly competitive, rapidly changing, and high pressure work environment.	

Total [ ]

Enterprising Careers: Summary Results

Compile your Enterprising Career Vector totals from the previous sections.

#5: Enterprising Career Vector	Section One: General Career-Related Interests and Preferences	Section Two: Occupations that Might Appeal to You	Section Three: Skills, Both Current and Potential	Section Four: Work-Related Personality/ Style Characteristics
Totals				

#6: Conventional Career Vector

Section One: General Career-Related Interests and Preferences

Please review the clusters of career-related interests and preferences below. Check the box provided if any of the interest activity statements appeal to you.

- If some but not all of the activities mentioned within each box interest you, check the box and underline the particular activities that appeal.

- Don't hold back just because you don't believe you have the skills, education or training needed to perform the activity. If the appeal is there, check the box. Even if you have never performed the activity, if you think you would enjoy it, check the box.

1. I am interested in practical business functions such as accounting, auditing, budget management, financial analysis, banking, quality control, and general administrative functions.	
2. I like to plan, organize, and coordinate schedules, systems, and operations and organize people, projects, and resources to accomplish tasks and goals.	
3. I enjoy working with numerical data and numbers and like compiling statistical information on spreadsheets.	
4. I enjoy working with business application computers and using the major business oriented software tools such as Microsoft Office Suite.	
5. I enjoy bringing systems, order, structure and organization to the workplace to enhance efficiency, productivity, data management, and keeping things organized and running smoothly.	
6. I am interested in banking and financial operations and would be interested in establishing an effective cost control and financial management system for an organization.	
7. I like keeping things organized and would like to develop an effective database system for a business organization or healthcare facility to store, organize, and manage data, records, and information.	
8. I like to plan, prepare, administer, and manage effective budgets and like to monitor, control, and manage cash flow, operating expenses, and revenues. I get satisfaction from improving the cost effectiveness of ongoing programs.	
9. I have an interest in financial analysis and enjoy analyzing financial information and preparing financial statements and reports.	
10. I like to organize things and would get satisfaction from helping people to organize their homes and offices more efficiently and manage their time more effectively.	
11. I would like to use my organizational skills as an administrator of an IT system or database. For example, I would like to be a web administrator for an organization.	

(continued on next page)

(continued from previous page)

12. I would like to maintain network and computer system security for an organization.	
13. I like gathering and structuring information and enjoy activities and roles involving the organization, practical use, and application of data and factual information for business purposes and/or to help people.	
14. I like developing and managing efficient systems and administrative procedures for getting things done and achieving business goals. For example, I would enjoy setting up a system to monitor and manage quality control for an organization.	
15. I enjoy and am good at activities requiring accuracy, precision, systematic approaches, thoroughness and attention to detail. I would be interested in meeting the accounting needs of individuals and organizations.	

Total

#6: Conventional Career Vector

Section Two: Occupations that Might Appeal to You

Check the box next to any occupation or occupational grouping that interests you. Don't be concerned about having the skills or experience required, only whether the occupation appeals to you.

• If some but not all of the occupations in one group interest you, check the box and underline the particular occupations that appeal.

1. College Registrar
   Museum Archivist/Museum Registrar
   Museum Curator	

2. Financial Analyst/Chartered Financial Analyst
   Banking Operations Specialist/Loan Officer
   Employee Compensation, Benefits, and Job Analysis Specialist	

3. Medical Insurance Specialist
   Insurance Claims Adjuster/Appraiser/Examiner/Investigator
   Insurance Underwriter	

4. Business Operations Specialist
   Administrative Assistant/Paralegal/Legal Assistant
   Court Reporter	

(continued on next page)

CareerVectors

5. Librarian/Library Assistant/Library Career Information Specialist Social and Human Services Assistant Social Science Research Assistant	
6. Judicial Law Clerk Internal Affairs Investigator Polygraph Examiner	
7. Accounting/Bookkeeping Teacher Business Computer Skills Instructor High School Business Education Teacher	
8. Professional Organizer Conference/Special Events/Meeting Coordinator Party/Wedding Planner	
9. Accountant/Tax/Cost Accountant/Auditor Budget Analyst Forensic Accounting Specialist	
10. Medical Records and Health Information Technician Clinical Data Manager Occupational Health and Safety Technician	
11. Mail Boxes Etc. Franchise Owner (provides business services including professional packaging, shipping, mail box rental, internet access, and copying services) Owner/Operator of a Medical Billing, Claims Processing and Collection Business Owner/Operator of an Office Products and Supplies Business	
12. Quality Control Coordinator Compliance Officer/Environmental Compliance Inspector Occupational Safety and Health Inspector	
13. Real Estate Appraiser Real Estate Title Examiner	
14. Computer Security Specialist/Coordinator Web Administrator/Database Administrator Desktop publisher/Website editor	
15. Financial Aid Counselor/Officer Investment Underwriter/Investment Analyst Brokerage House Administrative/Operations Specialist/Stock Transfer Clerk	

Total

Section Three: Skills, Both Current and Potential

We will be identifying both your current motivated skills (Areas of Effectiveness) and your potential skills (Skill Areas Reflecting a Potential for Development.)

Current Motivated Skills

Please *check the box* next to any skills cluster that contains a skill that you enjoy using, gain satisfaction from, and believe you can currently perform at least reasonably well.

Potential Skills

Please review the list of skills once more. This time, note if there are any skills listed that you have not had experience using, and do not currently possess but would like to develop, think you would enjoy using, and believe you could learn to perform at least reasonably well.

Note these skills by *putting a D in the box* next to any cluster of skills that contains a skill that you would like to develop according to the guidelines above, and underline the relevant skills.

IMPORTANT NOTES

Note that often each box contains a group or cluster of related skills. You need not possess them all. If you believe that any of the skills listed apply to you, please check the box and underline the relevant skills.

As you rate your skills, try not to be overly perfectionistic or think in all or nothing terms. Give yourself the benefit of the doubt if you are not sure.

It is possible to have checks and D's in the same cluster of skills. This would indicate that you believe certain skills within that cluster apply to you now, and that there are others within the same group of skills that you would like to develop.

1. Accounting, auditing, and budget administration and management skills. Tax accounting skills/income tax preparation skills. Forensic accounting skills. Can develop and maintain effective cost control and financial management systems.	
2. Banking operations, and credit analysis skills. Financial analysis skills: can analyze financial information and prepare financial reports. Brokerage house administrative skills including stock transfer skills.	
3. Information, data, and record management skills. Health information management/technology skills. Can keep accurate and up-to-date records and statistics.	
4. Organizational/administrative and business operations skills: can organize people, projects, data, and things. Can handle day-to-day operations and administrative details. Can plan, organize, structure, coordinate, and schedule work activities, tasks, and projects to accomplish organizational and professional goals. Can develop, monitor, and maintain efficient systems and procedures to get things done.	

(continued on next page)

5. Project management and administration skills: can bring projects in on time and within budget. Effective at planning and coordinating logistics: having the right things, at the right place, at the right time. Event planning and coordination skills.	
6. Insurance adjuster, claims examiner, and/or investigator skills. Insurance underwriter skills. Real estate appraisal and title search skills.	
7. Knowledge of health insurance concepts and practices including the new Affordable Care Act. Familiar with health insurance administrative procedures for processing claims.	
8. Time management skills: can plan organize, structure and manage time well. Can accurately assess the amount of time and effort needed to complete tasks and projects.	
9. Can research, gather, assemble and compile practical data, facts, and information. Can classify, organize, systematize, structure, and categorize data and information for practical use for business purposes and/or to help people.	
10. Effective quality control, quality assurance, and quality management skills.	
11. Strong business application computing skills: can effectively use the major business-oriented computer software tools such as Microsoft Office Suite.	
12. Web administration skills. Database administration skills—can manage, monitor, update and maintain databases. Computer information systems and network security skills.	
13. Strong numerical skills: can work well with numbers. Can use numerical data to analyze costs, prepare cost estimates, financial projections and comparisons.	
14. Administrative assistant skills. Paralegal skills: can assist lawyers with legal research and preparing legal documents.	
15. Librarian skills/librarian assistant skills. Social and human services assistant skills. Can assist clients in identifying available benefits and social and community services and help obtain them.	

Total [ ]

SCORING INSTRUCTIONS

When scoring, please do not count each box more than once. If there is a check and a (D) in the same box, please count only the one that gives you the most satisfaction.

To obtain your total score, please add up the number of boxes that contain a mark (either a check mark or a D mark) and enter your total.

Section Four: Work-Related Personality/Style Characteristics

Place a check next to any work-related personality pattern that fits with your perception of yourself. Note that not all of the traits have to apply, as long as you believe that some essential traits describe you reasonably well.

Next underline those characteristics that you believe fit you best.

1. I have a need for structure, stability, predictability, organization and efficiency. I like for things to be in order and like to have a place for everything, and everything in its place.	
2. When I work, I like to have things well planned and organized. I dislike ambiguity, lack of structure, open-ended situations, lack of closure, and disorganization.	
3. I can have difficulty being assertive and aggressive, and may, at times, be perceived as somewhat passive in my behavior.	
4. I am efficient, thorough, systematic, and detail-oriented in my approach to work and I like to know exactly what is expected of me.	
5. I am conscientious, reliable, responsible, steady, and dependable. I always try to be prepared and follow up on tasks in a timely manner. I manage my time well, am punctual, and can be counted on to meet deadlines.	
6. I can have difficulty dealing with and managing change, especially when the change is unplanned and unexpected.	
7. I relate well to authority figures and am comfortable taking direction from others and following company policies.	
8. I can be somewhat perfectionistic and compulsive. I have many "shoulds," and "oughts," and can be conforming, inhibited, controlled, and somewhat inflexible.	
9. I generally prefer working in a role other than a leadership or senior, general management role. I am comfortable in a subordinate role. My temperament and personality often fit best in a structured, support, operational, or administrative position. I am generally most comfortable working in a specialist or technical/functional role rather than as a generalist.	
10. I am not a risk-taker by nature and tend to be cautious, deliberate, conservative, and traditional. I have a need for certainty, security, and prefer the known, predictable, and familiar. My overly cautious nature and fear of change can interfere with appropriate risk-taking, creativity, innovation, and adaptability to change and market needs. I am concerned that this can limit my potential for business and/or professional success.	

(continued on next page)

11. I like to be careful, accurate and precise, and make sure things are done right. I value planning, preparation and organization and I find it stressful when I have to rush through my work or engage in last-minute preparation.	
12. I am inclined to be practical, specific, and applied rather than imaginative, creative, and abstract. I can get bogged down in detail and not see the big picture.	
13. I have a strong need for control, try to keep my emotions under control, and seek to regulate and control my life as much as possible. I try to reduce stress by planning ahead and like to make lists of things to do.	
14. External structure provides an important degree of comfort and security for me. I derive a sense of security from systems, routines, clear-cut guidelines, rules, and operating procedures.	
15. I like structure and classification systems because they satisfy my need for order and practical application. They can be applied and put to practical use for business purposes and/or to help people.	

Total [ ]

Conventional Careers: Summary Results

Compile your Conventional Career Vector totals from the previous sections.

#6: Conventional Career Vector	Section One: General Career-Related Interests and Preferences	Section Two: Occupations that Might Appeal to You	Section Three: Skills, Both Current and Potential	Section Four: Work-Related Personality/ Style Characteristics
Totals				

CVS Summary of Results

Look back at the end of each Career Vector scale to the Summary tables to find the total number of items checked from each section. Please enter your numbers in the chart below, and add up your results.

	#1 Realistic Vector	#2 Investigative Vector	#3 Artistic Vector	#4 Social Vector	#5 Enterprising Vector	#6 Conventional Vector
Section One: General Career-Related Interests and Preferences						
Section Two: Occupations that Might Appeal to You						
Section Three: Skills, Both Current and Potential						
Section Four: Work-Related Personality/ Style Characteristics						
Totals						

List your three highest scores below. In the event of a tie, choose the Vector that seems most like you.

_____   _____   _____

Highest Vector Score   2nd Highest Vector Score   3rd Highest Vector Score

CVS Summary Profiles

At the end of the CVS self-assessment process, you will have identified major factors that relate to your career success and satisfaction including your major work related strengths and development needs, occupational preferences, and personality characteristics.

The following summary profiles are provided for you to have a record of your assessment results that you can use as you plan and manage your career.

CVS Summary Profile
Section One: General Career-Related Interests and Preferences

From Section One of the CVS, please prioritize a list of up to fifteen of your strongest career-related interest patterns.

1 _____

2 _____

3 _____

4 _____

5 _____

6 _____

7 _____

8 _____

9 _____

10 _____

11 _____

12 _____

13 _____

14 _____

15 _____

CVS Summary Profile

CVS Summary Profile
Section Two: Occupations of Interest

Section Two of the CVS contains a group of fifteen clusters of occupations related to each Career Vector area. Please prioritize up to fifteen occupations of interest that you may wish to explore further.

1 _____

2 _____

3 _____

4 _____

5 _____

6 _____

7 _____

8 _____

9 _____

10 _____

11 _____

12 _____

13 _____

14 _____

15 _____

CVS Summary Profile

CVS Summary Profile
Section Three: CURRENT Motivated Skills
(Areas Of Effectiveness)

Your current motivated skills are those that you gain satisfaction from using and believe you can currently perform at least reasonably well.

From Section Three, please read through the list of skills and identify up to fifteen skills that you currently enjoy using and believe you can do at least reasonably well. Next, try to prioritize these skills below according to the degree of satisfaction you gain from using each one.

1 _____

2 _____

3 _____

4 _____

5 _____

6 _____

7 _____

8 _____

9 _____

10 _____

11 _____

12 _____

13 _____

14 _____

15 _____

CVS Summary Profile

CVS Summary Profile
Section Three: POTENTIAL Skills:
Skill Areas Reflecting a Potential for Development

These are the skills that you may not have had experience using and currently do not possess, but would like to develop, feel you would enjoy using, and believe you can learn to perform at least reasonably well.

Please review your list of potential skills (those marked with a D) that you identified, and list up to fifteen potential skills that you would like to develop in prioritized order (according to degree of satisfaction).

1 _____

2 _____

3 _____

4 _____

5 _____

6 _____

7 _____

8 _____

9 _____

10 _____

11 _____

12 _____

13 _____

14 _____

15 _____

CVS Introduction to Personality Section

Introduction to Section Four:
Work-Related Personality/Style Characteristics

Recognition and understanding of one's work-related personality characteristics is critically important in the career development process. The sections that follow from Section Four will help you summarize various important aspects of your work-related personality characteristics and traits as revealed in your Career Vector preferences. These include your work-related behavioral patterns and tendencies, your core career needs (motivators), your adaptive/self-management traits, and your preferred style of operating and working.

Each of the six Career Vectors is associated with both positive and potentially problematic, maladaptive, and negative personality traits and characteristics.

CVS Summary Profile

CVS Summary Profile
Section Four: <u>Positive</u> Work-Related Personality/Style Characteristics and Traits

Please review the personality statements you checked in Section Four, and list up to 15 <u>positive</u> work-related personality traits in prioritized order, that you believe you possess and that describe the way you typically function at work.

1 _____

2 _____

3 _____

4 _____

5 _____

6 _____

7 _____

8 _____

9 _____

10 _____

11 _____

12 _____

13 _____

14 _____

15 _____

CVS Summary Profile

Section Four: Potentially Problematic, <u>Negative</u> Work-Related Personality/Style Characteristics and Traits

Finally, please read through the list of personality traits again, and this time, identify and make a list below of those potentially problematic, maladaptive, or <u>negative</u> traits that you believe you possess and that could potentially interfere with your work effectiveness, and/or satisfaction. Include those traits that you would like to develop, improve, modify, or learn to cope with and manage more effectively.

Prioritize a list of up to fifteen <u>negative</u> personality traits you would most like to work on and improve:

1 _____

2 _____

3 _____

4 _____

5 _____

6 _____

7 _____

8 _____

9 _____

10 _____

11 _____

12 _____

13 _____

14 _____

15 _____

Concluding Remarks

It is our hope that with the expanded self and occupational knowledge gained from completing the CVS, you will be better able to make more informed and satisfying career-related decisions.

If you feel the need for additional assistance, we encourage you to consider working with a professional career counselor who can help guide you through the career development process, help you to better understand and apply your CVS results, and assist you with any specific career-related needs and concerns you may have.

Please refer to *www.NCDA.org* for information about services that career counselors provide and how to find one.

For more information about the CVS, please see our website at www.careervectors.net.

If you would like to contact the developers of the CVS, please feel free to email them at Hope@careervectors.net.

Our very best wishes for success and satisfaction in your future life/work/career endeavors.

—Barry Lustig and Hope Lovell Newman

Professional Biographies

Barry Lustig, M.A., Prof. Dipl.
Developer of the Career Vectors System

Barry Lustig, formerly the director of the Career Assessment Institute of Federation Employment and Guidance Services (a large New York Human Service Agency), is a Career Assessment and Development Specialist with over 45 years of professional experience.

He has had a longtime interest in the training and development of career counselors. He created and directed the F.E.G.S. Professional Development Institute, a training program for career counselors and related professions that also provided consultation and training to human resource departments of organizations, career development and outplacement firms, and colleges and universities.

Barry was an adjunct instructor at the New School (Milano Division) Human Resources Management graduate program for approximately 20 years. He developed their Adult Career Development and Counseling Certificate Program which was a graduate program consisting of a comprehensive coverage (eight courses) of all aspects of the career counseling field.

Prior to that, he had developed the first career counseling certificate program in New York with Queens College (School of Continuing Education) and F.E.G.S. He has also taught courses in career counseling and career assessment as an adjunct instructor at Pace University, Teacher's College, Columbia University, and New York University School of Continuing Education.

Barry has had a special interest in career assessment and created the F.E.G.S. Comprehensive Career Assessment Model to provide an in-depth assessment process that includes addressing the multi-faceted aspects of personality as major components of career development, competency and effectiveness.

Using this assessment model, he has worked with many individuals whose career confusion was symptomatic of self-confusion, and who were in need of developing greater insight and clarity into their self/career identity profile. This led to his contributing to the book *If You Knew Who You Were, You Could Be Who You Are,* by Dr. Gerald Sturman.

Barry developed and recently revised the Career Vectors System, a career assessment instrument that integrates the assessment of vocational interests, skills and abilities, and work-related personality characteristics, helping individuals to understand their strengths and development needs and identify possible career directions to explore.

He has also created a comprehensive career assessment card sort, "The Strengths and Development Needs Card Sort," which includes an assessment of functional skills and competencies, preferred work roles, adaptive/self-management traits, and internal barriers. The card sort can be used in both career counseling and executive coaching.

(continued on next page)

(continued from previous page)

He has been a career assessment and testing consultant to colleges and universities, human resource consulting and psychological testing firms. Additionally, he has been the career assessment content and subject matter consultant to various publications including the book, *The Career Discovery Project,* (published by Doubleday) also by Dr. Sturman.

Barry also has a strong interest in clinical and psychological issues in career counseling and originated the use of the term, "Clinical Career Counseling" in New York. This involves the exploration, assessment, and management of personality factors and internal barriers that can negatively affect one's career development and interfere with career success and satisfaction.

He has written a monograph, "Personality Dynamics and Internal Barriers in Clinical Career Counseling and Executive Coaching," and has taught courses on this subject at F.E.G.S., and the New School for many years. He has also made several presentations and conducted workshops on this and related topics including the use of personality assessment techniques in career counseling.

Barry received his B.A. degree in Psychology from Queens College (CUNY) and an M.A. in Vocational Guidance from New York University. He also received a Professional Diploma from Teacher's College, Columbia University in Student Personnel Administration in Higher Education with a concentration of course work in Counseling Psychology.

Hope Lovell Newman, L.M.S.W.
President, Career Vectors, L.L.C.

Hope Lovell Newman, L.M.S.W., has a passion to help people find emotionally rewarding and meaningful work. She met Barry while counseling students at the New School as a Career Counselor. Hope recognized the value of Career Vectors as a tool to help clients who are in need of career direction to gain an increased understanding of themselves and find a career in line with their values, interests, skills, abilities, and personality.

Hope spent many years in career distress herself and has great compassion and empathy for people struggling to find or change career paths. She formed Career Vectors, L.L.C. in June 2013 out of a desire to help people by providing them with tools for both comprehensive self assessment and the translation of that into the identification of occupational possibilities to explore that are related to the current job market.

She currently works as a Career Counselor at the Milano School of International Affairs, Management, and Urban Policy, a division of the New School.

Hope graduated with honors from Brown University, and has an MA degree from Columbia University, and an MSW degree from Hunter College School of Social Work. She also completed graduate work in Career Counseling and Career Assessment at Fordham University Graduate School of Education. Hope is very grateful to her wonderful family for their support. She is also deeply indebted to Barry Lustig for his encouragement and commitment to carrying out this project with her.